INSIDE MAGIC

PRESTO CHANGE-O!
JAW-DROPPING MAGIC WITH DINNER TABLE OBJECTS

Nicholas Einhorn

New York

This edition published in 2013 by:

The Rosen Publishing Group, Inc.
29 East 21st Street
New York, NY 10010

Library of Congress Cataloging-in-Publication Data

Einhorn, Nicholas.
Presto change-o!: jaw-dropping magic with dinner table objects/Nicholas Einhorn.
    p. cm.—(Inside magic)
Includes bibliographical references (p.   ) and index.
ISBN 978-1-4488-9220-4 (library binding)
1. Magic tricks—Juvenile literature. I. Title.
GV1548.E333 2013
793.8—dc23

                                                                                    2012029046

Manufactured in the United States of America

CPSIA Compliance Information: Batch #W13YA: For further information, contact Rosen Publishing, New York, New York, at 1-800-237-9932.

Copyright in design, text and images © Anness Publishing Limited, U.K. 2002, 2013. Originally published as part of a larger volume: *The Art of Magic*.

CONTENTS

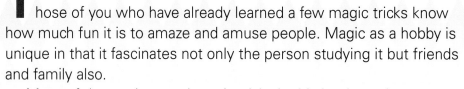

INTRODUCTION

Those of you who have already learned a few magic tricks know how much fun it is to amaze and amuse people. Magic as a hobby is unique in that it fascinates not only the person studying it but friends and family also.

Many of the routines and magic tricks in this book can be performed at a moment's notice with whatever objects happen to be lying around. If you take the time to learn a few clever routines, you will be able to entertain and astound people at any time. Most of these tricks can be performed without any setup, and many of the items you require can be found on a dinner table or at a restaurant.

The dinner table is an ideal place to perform magic for your friends and family. Glasses, napkins, utensils, straws, cups and sugar cubes are just some of the objects often found on tables at mealtimes. It is a good idea to learn some magic tricks with these items so that whenever you eat with other people you are in a position to entertain. An ordinary dinner or gathering can become a very memorable occasion with an impromptu performance, and if the guests do not know each other, magic is an ideal icebreaker. You can be sure that your performance will lead to conversation and no doubt speculation as to how you achieved your miracles.

The following pages also explain a variety of tricks using string, cord and rope. You will soon be able to cut and restore them, make them pass through human flesh and make knots mysteriously disappear at will. A staple of many magicians' repertoires is the "cut and restored" rope effect. A length of rope is cut into two—sometimes three—pieces and caused to restore itself. There are dozens of methods in existence, and several are explained in this book.

Finally, in the following pages you will learn how to create the impression of mind reading and even of being able to predict future events. Scientists have long subscribed to the belief that humans use only a fraction of their potential brainpower. Many people believe we have, and some even claim to have, a sixth sense with which to read people's minds and make predictions about forthcoming events. Do paranormal powers really exist? People will believe they do when you show them some of the routines in this book.

You are taking the time to learn something that can make you memorable and popular for all the right reasons. If you keep the secrets, the secrets will keep you.

rolling straw

A straw is set on the table in front of you, and you then rub a fingertip against your sleeve. As you hold your finger above the straw, it rolls forward as if repelled by a magnetic force. The best kind of straw to use is the type that is supplied free in fast-food restaurants.

As will become apparent when you read through the method to this trick, it may be a good idea to fail a few times before finally succeeding. Your audience will become accustomed to watching you rub your finger on your sleeve, and this will provide you with perfect misdirection.

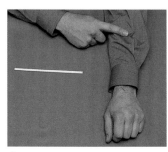

1. Place a straw in front of you on the table, and rub your first finger on your sleeve. Explain that you are generating static electricity.

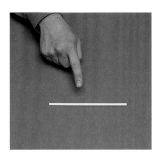

2. Hold your finger directly above the straw.

3. Move your finger forward, and as you do so, secretly blow at the table in front of the straw. The breeze will cause the straw to roll forward. Try not to change the shape of your face as you blow; all eyes should be on your finger.

clinging cutlery

This is a perfect dinner table stunt. It is easy to perform, yet completely mystifying. A fork is made to cling to the outstretched palm of your hand. The secret is explained, but moments later it is revealed that you were not being entirely honest, as the fork is once again made to cling to your hand in an even more amazing fashion! The setup takes just a few seconds.

Secret View

1. Hold a fork in your closed left fist. Grip your left wrist with your right hand and open the left fingers wide. The right first finger secretly stretches out to hold the fork in place.

2. From the front, it looks as if the fork is stuck to your hand. You can stop the illusion here, but you can also go a step further. Turn your hands around, exposing the method to the trick. Return to the same position.

3. The right hand is now removed completely, yet the fork still stays suspended from the left hand. How?

Secret View

4. This exposed view shows how a knife is held under your watch-band from the start. When you pretend to reveal your secret, the knife is covered by your first finger (see step 1).

bending knife (version 1)

A knife is held between the fingertips and gently shaken up and down. The metal seems to turn to rubber, and the illusion is created of the knife bending. This illusion also works with rulers, nails, pens and many other objects. It is the perfect effect to show just before the even more impressive Bending Knife (Version 2), described next.

This optical illusion dates back a long way and is a good example of "retention of vision." This is the term used to describe an effect in which an image remains in view for a few moments after it has been moved away.

At about chest level, hold a knife loosely at one end, between the thumb and first finger of the right hand. Quickly and continuously move your right hand up and down about 4 in (10 cm). As the knife begins to shake, it appears to become wobbly, as if made of rubber.

bending knife (version 2)

This is a great follow-up to Version 1. A knife is bent in half at right angles, then straightened out again. The optical illusion is perfect.

It is not necessary to use a coin, as seen below, because the trick works almost as well without it, but the coin does give conviction to the illusion.

Secret View

1. Hold a knife in the right hand with the tip against the table. The fourth finger should rest behind the handle and the other fingers in front. Hold a coin at the top of the knife between the finger and thumb. Only the tip of the coin is seen, and it is mistaken by the observer for the top of the knife.

2. The left hand closes around the right hand as shown. The knife is supported entirely by the right hand. The left hand simply helps to hide the method.

3. The knife is pushed against the table. Although the hands stay straight, the knife is allowed to fall flat, pivoting between the right third and fourth fingers, as seen in this exposed view.

4. From the front, with both hands covering the method, this is how the illusion looks. Finish by raising the hands, therefore straightening the knife and showing that it has unbent itself.

bouncing bread roll

A bread roll is picked up off the table and apparently bounced on the floor, like a tennis ball. It shoots up into the air, and you catch it as if it were the most natural thing in the world. This trick would work equally well with a piece of fruit such as an apple or orange, and even a pool ball at a pool table! As long as you use an object that would not ordinarily bounce, the effect will register well.

1. This trick is easiest to do sitting at a table, although once you understand the principle you can also do it standing. Hold a bread roll in your right hand, at about shoulder height.

2. Bring your hand down below the table's edge, exactly as if you were about to bounce the roll onto the floor.

3. As soon as your hand passes the edge of the table it will be out of sight. This is where you have to work with split-second timing if the illusion is to be a success. Notice how the foot is ready to tap against the floor, simulating the sound of the roll hitting the ground.

4. The moment the hand is below the table's edge, it turns at the wrist and flicks the roll up into the air as straight as possible. There should be no movement from the arm itself; only the wrist should move. A split second before you toss the roll, tap your foot on the ground.

5. Follow the movement of the roll with your head. The combination of sounds and visuals will provide the perfect illusion of the bread roll bouncing.

vanishing glass

In this amazing impromptu trick, a coin is covered with a glass, which in turn is covered with a paper napkin. While the audience's attention is focused on the coin, the glass is somehow made to disappear. You can also make it pass straight through the top of the table.

1. Perform this sitting at a table. Place a coin on the table in front of you, then place a glass, mouth down, on top of it. Cover the glass with a paper napkin from the top downwards so that the paper is stretched around the top and sides and would hold its shape even if the glass were removed; the bottom should remain open. Ask a spectator if the coin on the table is heads up or tails up.

2. Lift the covered glass up and back towards the edge of the table with one hand, exposing the coin. Bring attention to the coin by pointing to it with the other hand. This is simply misdirection to divert the attention of the spectators away from what happens next.

Secret View

3. The glass should be resting on the edge of the table in front of you. Allow it to slip out of the napkin and safely onto your lap. There is no "move" as such – simply lift the glass away from the coin and allow it to fall silently. The napkin will hold its shape, so a casual glance should not arouse any suspicion.

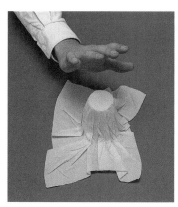

4. Carefully place the napkin shell back over the coin and remove your hand.

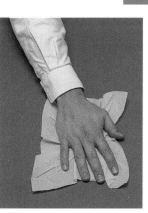

5. Tell the audience to watch as you proceed to smash the "glass" flat to the table under your hand. This sudden noise will create the moment of impact you should strive for. One moment the glass is there, and the next it has completely disappeared!

tip As a variation, ask the spectator to hold his hand out just above the "glass." Place your hand above his and bring your hand down onto his as the paper is flattened. This directly involves the spectator, who is expecting to feel the glass. Instead of creating the illusion of the glass disappearing, you can also finish by telling the audience that the glass went straight through the table. Simply produce the glass from beneath. If a glass is not available, you can do the same trick with a saltshaker or pepper grinder.

torn and restored napkin

A paper napkin is torn into small pieces and squeezed between the hands. The pieces magically weld themselves together again. The napkins in the photographs are shown in different colors for ease of explanation.

A little experimentation with napkins will reveal that the paper is easy to tear in one direction because of the direction of the grain. Try to orient the napkins correctly when you set up this trick so that the tearing is made easier for you.

1. To prepare, apply a small amount of glue to the top right corner of a paper napkin (at the point here marked "X").

2. Glue a second napkin to the first at this point. Wait for the glue to dry.

3. Scrunch up the top napkin into a ball. Neatness is not important.

4. Continue to squeeze the ball, making it as small as possible. You are now ready to start performing the trick.

Secret View

5. Hold the flat napkin in both hands so that the duplicate ball is at the top right corner on your side of the paper. Begin to tear the napkin in half down the center.

6. From the front, the duplicate ball is hidden completely and must remain so. The napkin provides lots of cover.

Secret View

7. Place the left half of the napkin in front of the right half. Tear the paper down the center as before.

8. Place the left pieces in front of the right and then turn the strip sideways so that you can tear the strip down the center.

Secret View

9. Place the left pieces in front of the right again, and then make one final tear down the center.

10. Place the final pieces of paper in front of the right-hand pieces as before and squeeze the edges together.

Secret View

11. While you are squeezing the napkins, secretly turn them over so that the duplicate napkin is facing the front. As the real napkins are the same color, this move will be invisible.

12. Start to open up the napkin along the top edge, smoothing out the wrinkles as you go.

13. Continue to straighten it out until the entire napkin is revealed to be restored.

Secret View

14. The torn pieces are safely hidden behind the duplicate napkin at the top right corner. To finish, crumple all the paper into a ball and discard it.

sugar rush

This is a very popular effect in magic that is also known as "matrix." Four sugar cubes are set out in a square formation. Two playing cards are shown and used to cover the cubes briefly. The sugar cubes jump around, seemingly of their own free will, until they all meet in one corner. This is similar to the next routine, Sugar Rush Uncovered, but it does not require difficult sleight of hand because of the extra cover created by the two cards. If no playing cards are available, you could also perform the trick using coasters or even menus – whatever is at hand. If you learn both routines, you will have a nice set piece to perform at a dinner table.

1. Set out four sugar cubes in a square formation. The cubes should be about 12 in (30 cm) away from each other.

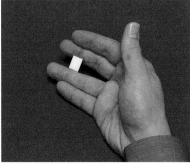

2. Grip an extra sugar cube between your second and third fingers, as shown. In performance, there will always be a card on top of your fingers so this cube will remain hidden.

3. Hold a playing card in each hand, so that they both look the same and the extra sugar cube cannot be seen. Cover both the upper right and left cubes.

Secret View

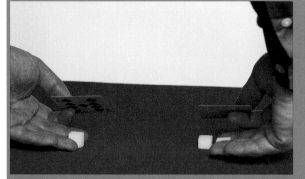

4. This exposed view shows how the right hand is about to let go of the hidden sugar cube while the left hand is getting ready to take a cube away under the card.

5. Move both cards to show that one cube has supposedly jumped. (Be careful not to expose the hidden sugar cube.)

6. Cover the upper right and the lower right cubes, repeating the same move as before. Both hands should move together and at a constant pace.

7. Move the hands back to show that a second cube has moved across to join the others. Do not pause for long, but continue to move your hands to the next position.

8. Cover the upper right and lower left corners, in preparation for the final sugar cube to travel.

9. Repeat the move one last time and show that all the sugar cubes are together at the top right corner.

sugar rush uncovered

Four sugar cubes are placed in a square formation on the table. The hands cover the cubes for a brief moment, and they start to jump from corner to corner until all four cubes join together in one corner. This routine is a perfect follow-up to Sugar Rush. The order of moves is basically the same, but instead of using cards as cover, this version relies entirely on a convincing classic palm. Palming a sugar cube is as easy as palming gets, which is why sugar cubes are ideal for this trick. You could also use upturned bottle caps, which are equally easy to palm because of their shape and easy-to-grip edges. In order to achieve success with this effect, some dedicated practice is required.

Secret View

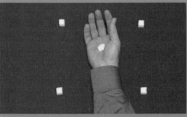

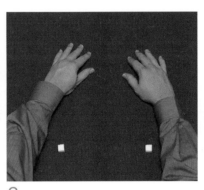

1. For this trick you will need a bowl of sugar cubes. Take five cubes from the bowl, secretly palming one in the right hand. Set the bowl off to your left-hand side, and set out the remaining four cubes in a square formation in front of you.

2. Cover the farthest two cubes with your hands. As you will notice, the sequence of moves is similar to that of Sugar Rush, so once you are familiar with that trick, this one will be easier to learn.

Secret View

3. Drop the palmed cube in your right hand, and palm the one under your left hand. This should take no more than a second, and both moves must happen simultaneously. With practice, you will be able to palm and drop the cubes without any noticeable movement from the back of your hand.

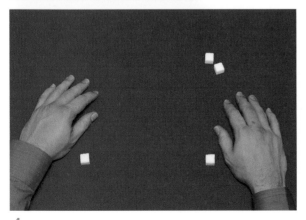

4. Move both hands away to reveal that one of the cubes appears to have jumped.

5. Without hesitation, cover the top right corner with your left hand and the bottom right corner with your right hand. Do the same move again, dropping the left-hand cube and picking up the cube at the lower right in a right-hand palm.

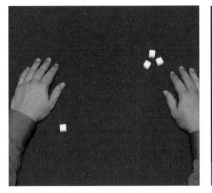

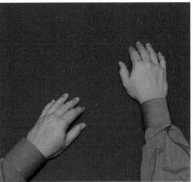

6. Move your hands to show that the second cube has moved.

7. Finally, cover the top right corner with your right hand and the bottom left corner with your left hand.

8. Perform the move one more time to show that all cubes are now at the top right corner.

Secret View

9. You will finish with a sugar cube palmed in the left hand. This is easy to get rid of. Simply pick up the sugar bowl to your left-hand side, and as you lift the bowl up, allow the cube to fall in, along with the other cubes.

10. Pick up the remaining cubes on the table and openly drop them back into the sugar bowl. The great thing about this routine is that you finish completely "clean"; that is, you destroy the evidence of the extra cube when you drop it back into the bowl.

all sugared up

A number is chosen at random and written on the side of a sugar cube. The cube is then dissolved in a glass of water and the written image is made to appear on the palm of the person who chose the number. You will need to use a very soft pencil and a sugar cube that is smooth on all sides. This routine will cause massive reactions because the effect actually happens in the spectator's hands.

Secret View

1 Before you begin the trick, secretly dip your right second finger into a glass of water to moisten it. If the liquid is cold, you may be able to moisten your finger by touching the condensation on the outside of the glass. Either way, you must ensure there is some moisture on your fingertip.

2. Ask a spectator to choose a number. Using a pencil, clearly print the number on one side of a sugar cube.

3. Squeeze the cube between your right thumb and second finger as your left hand moves the glass into view. The written number should be pressed against the moist second finger. Drop the cube into the water.

Secret View

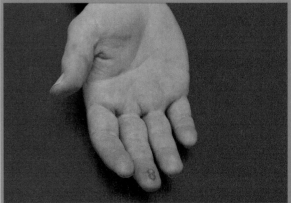

4. You have secretly transferred the graphite in the pencil to your fingertip. Now you must secretly transfer this to the palm of the person who chose the number.

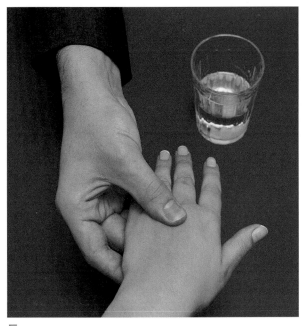

5. Ask her to hold out her hand, and then take hold of it and move it to a position above the glass. As you do so, lightly press your second finger against her palm.

6. This will transfer the image without her knowledge. The spectator should not notice because you are touching her for a reason, that is, under the pretense of repositioning her hand.

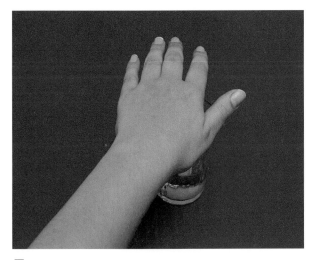

7. Ask the spectator to move her hand up and down above the glass. Explain what is going to happen: "As the sugar cube dissolves, the graphite will float to the surface of the water and the heat of your hand will cause the particles of graphite to turn into a vapor that will rise from the glass and attach itself to the palm of your hand."

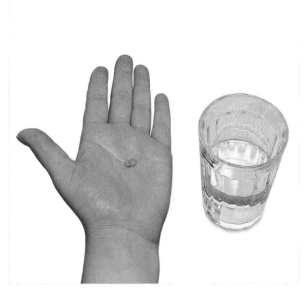

8. Ask the spectator to turn her hand palm up, and she will see the duplication of her number, drawn on the sugar cube moments before.

two in the hand

Three sugar cubes are displayed. Two are put into the left hand and one is placed in the magician's pocket, yet there are still three cubes in the left hand. This little mystery is repeated several times, culminating in the disappearance of all three!

If you enjoy this type of magic, then it may be worth investing in some magicians' sponge balls from a magic shop. They are quite inexpensive and come in a variety of different sizes and colors. They are the ideal prop to use for sleight of hand such as this, although you will find that it is also possible to use other small objects for an impromptu performance.

Secret View

1. Place three sugar cubes in a row on the table and have an extra cube secretly hidden in your right-hand finger palm. This cube must remain hidden throughout.

2. Pick up the cube at the far right and display it in the right fingertips. Hold out your left hand flat and count "One," placing the cube in your left palm.

3. Display the second sugar cube in the right fingertips and count "Two."

Secret View

4. As the second cube is placed into the hand, drop the extra cube along with it.

Secret View

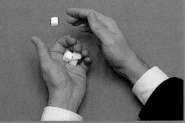

5. Immediately close the left hand and say, "Two sugar cubes in my left hand."

6. Say "One in the pocket." Suiting your action to these words, pick up the remaining cube from the table. Display it and pretend to put it in your right jacket pocket, but secretly retain it using a right finger palm.

7. Ask how many cubes are in your left hand and the response should be "Two." Say "Close!" as your left hand sets out the three cubes in a row on the table. Repeat steps 1 to 7; however, at step 6 really place the cube in your pocket and leave it there.

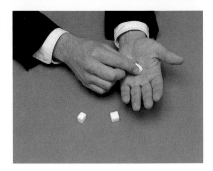

8. The third time, change the routine slightly. Pick up the cube at the far right and place it onto your left palm. Count "One."

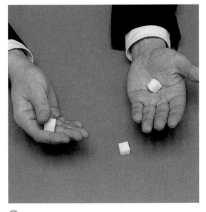

9. Pick up the second cube and display it in your fingers as before.

10. Count "Two" as you supposedly place this in your left hand along with the first cube. Continue your patter by saying, "Two cubes go into my left hand."

11. What you actually do is secretly pick up both cubes by pinching them against your fingers with your thumb. There must be no hesitation.

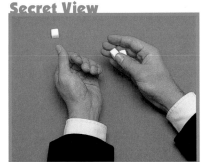

12. As the right hand comes away with the two hidden cubes, the left hand closes as if it still contains them.

13. Pick up and display the third cube. Say "One in the pocket," but in fact place all three cubes in your pocket.

14. Ask how many cubes are in your hand. The audience may assume two, or even three.

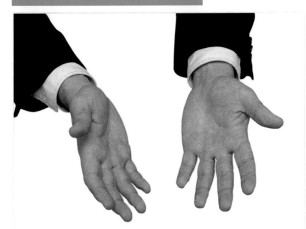

15. Open your left hand, showing that both your hands are completely empty and all of the sugar cubes have mysteriously disappeared!

16. This trick will work with a variety of small objects. You could, for example, tear up a paper napkin and roll the pieces into small balls. As mentioned in the introduction, magicians' sponge balls are also perfect for this trick.

knife and paper trick

Paper spots are stuck to the blade of a knife on both sides. The spots are removed, but they reappear at the magician's command. The sleight taught here has been used by magicians for decades and is still popular today. It includes the Paddle Move, which involves showing the same surface of an object twice while the spectator thinks they are seeing two different sides. This move has many applications.

1. Tear off six tiny pieces of paper from the corner of a paper napkin.

2. Dip the tip of your finger into a glass of water, and then touch the blade of the knife to transfer the drop of liquid.

3. Repeat this at two more points on the knife, and then place a paper spot on each wet point – the water makes them stick.

4. To practice the sleight you will use throughout this trick, hold the knife between your fingers and thumb with the blade pointing downwards. The paper should be on the top side of the blade.

5. Twist your wrist towards you so that the knife turns over and the blank side can be shown to the spectator.

6. Twist your wrist back again, reversing the action of step 5.

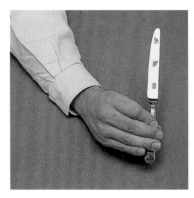

7. Repeat this wrist action once more, but as your wrist turns over, push the handle of the knife with your thumb so that the knife turns over at the same time as your hand. This time the spots will appear to be on the back of the knife as well. This is the Paddle Move. Turn your wrist back again, using the Paddle Move to flip the knife over at the same time.

8. To proceed with the trick, after step 3 add three more pieces of paper to the blank side of the knife. This completes the preparation.

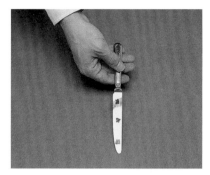

9. Now that you are familiar with the Paddle Move, you are ready to learn the sequence of moves for the routine. Display the knife in the right fingertips as shown.

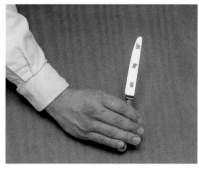

10. Twist the wrist (without performing the Paddle Move) and show three spots of paper on the other side of the knife blade.

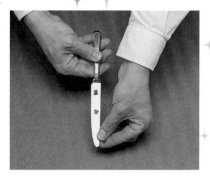

11. Bring the knife back to the start position and pull off the lowest spot. Pretend to slide off the spot on the underside of the knife at the same time.

12. Perform the Paddle Move, which allows you to show that the spot on the underside has also apparently been taken.

13. Repeat these moves with the second spot, in fact only taking the spot off the top of the knife.

14. Execute the Paddle Move again to show that both spots have supposedly been taken.

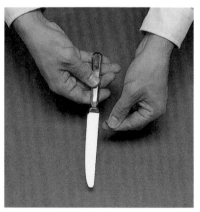

15. Repeat once more for the last spot remaining on the knife.

16. Using the Paddle Move, show that both sides of the knife are now blank.

17. With a shake of the wrist, quickly twist the knife between your fingers and thumb to make all three spots reappear. These can be shown to be apparently on both sides, using the Paddle Move one last time. Finish by removing the three spots, thus destroying the evidence.

the cups and balls

It has been said that a magician's abilities can be measured by the performance of this great trick, of which there are many versions. Some use just one cup, others two or three, but the effect is always similar. A number of small balls are caused to vanish, penetrate and reappear under the cup or cups, often changing into fruit and even live mice and chicks along the way! This basic version uses three balls and three cups. It is easy to perform and amazing to watch. Professional sets of the cups and balls are available from magic shops.

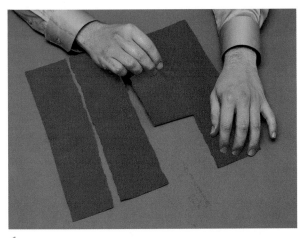

1. You will require four small ball-like objects. You can use sugar cubes for an impromptu performance, or you can fashion balls from a paper napkin torn into four strips.

2. Roll each strip into a ball. Although you will be using four balls, the audience will only ever be aware of three of them.

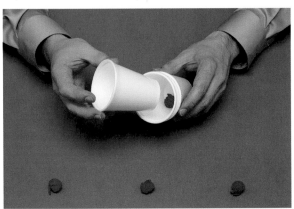

3. Stack three cups together, hiding a ball in the center cup. Set the other three balls in a row in front of you. You are now ready to perform the incredible Cups and Balls.

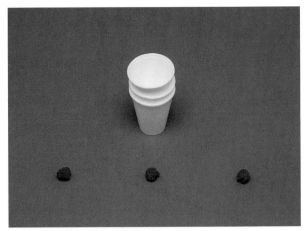

4. This shows the preparation completed and is how the cups should be set before you begin the routine.

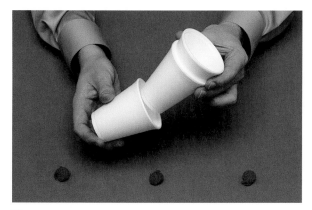

5. Pick up all three cups in a stack with your left hand. The right hand takes the bottom cup from underneath and pulls it off the stack. Keep the mouth of the cup away from the spectator.

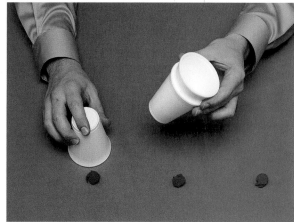

6. Turn this cup upside down next to the ball on your far right, as shown above.

7. Repeat step 6 with the second cup. Although there is a ball hidden inside this second cup, it will remain unseen and will not fall out if the cup is turned at a constant speed.

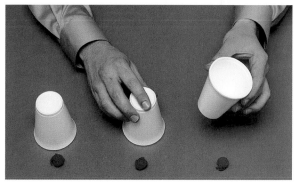

8. Place the second cup next to the center ball, with the secret ball hidden beneath it. You must practice this until you can position the cup without fear of the extra ball falling out.

9. Finally, turn over the third cup and place it next to the ball at the far left. The extra ball is hidden under the middle cup.

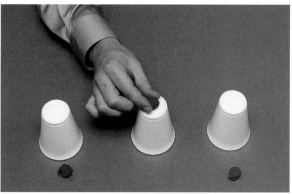

10. Pick up the center ball and place it on the bottom of the middle cup. ▶

11. Stack the outer two cups on top of the center one. Make a magical gesture, and then tilt back the stack of cups to show that the ball has apparently penetrated the center cup and is now on the table. Pause to let this effect register with your audience.

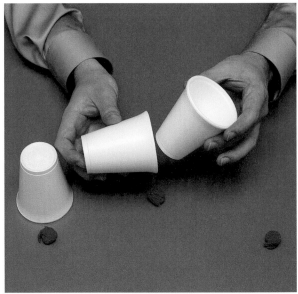

12. Pick up the stack of cups and turn them mouth upwards again. Now repeat the set of moves and turn each cup over again. Place the first cup at the right, next to the ball. Place the second cup (containing the extra ball) over the center ball.

13. The third cup goes next to the ball on the left. Pick up the right ball and place it on top of the middle cup. This sequence of moves is almost identical to the sequence at the start of the routine.

14. Stack the other two cups on top as before. Make a magical gesture above the cups.

15 Tilt the cups back to show that the second ball has joined the first.

16 Repeat the moves one final time. Place the first cup to the right, the second cup over the balls already on the table, and the third cup to the left.

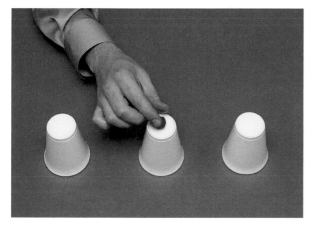

17 Pick up the last remaining ball and place it on the underside of the center cup (see Tip for an alternative move).

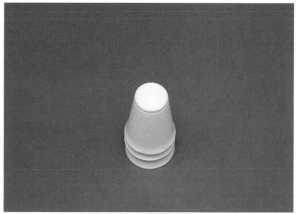

18 Stack the cups one last time and make another magical gesture over them.

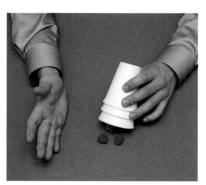

19 Tilt the cups back to reveal all three balls together.

20 That is the mystery of the Cups and Balls!

tip When you reach step 17, instead of placing the final ball on the cup you can "vanish" it using any technique that you are familiar with. The final ball will then be shown to have magically reappeared under the final cup.

cut and re-strawed

A long piece of string is threaded through a straw, which is then bent in half. The straw and string are cut through the middle and displayed in two pieces, but when the string is removed from the straw, it has magically restored itself! The best straws to use are those found in fast-food restaurants. The only preparation required is a slit that must be cut and that will remain hidden by the stripes on the straw.

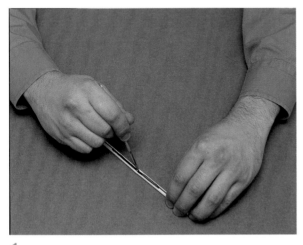

1. To prepare, carefully cut a slit in a drinking straw, using a scalpel. The slit should not go all the way to the ends. It is seen as a black line here for ease of explanation.

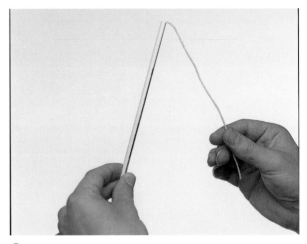

2. Hold the straw so that the slit is facing towards you and therefore hidden from anyone viewing from the front. Thread a string through the straw so that a piece hangs from each end.

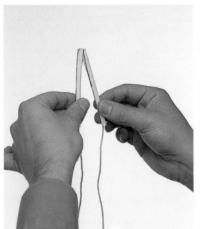

3. Hold one end of the straw in each hand and bend it in half so that the slit is on the inside.

Secret View

4. Hold the straw in the left fingertips and pull the ends so that the middle of the string slips out of the slit and behind the left first finger. Pinch the string together with the straw between the left first finger and the thumb.

5. Cut the straw neatly in two. The middle of the string remains hidden, but the illusion created is that both the string and the straw have been cut.

6. From the front, it can be seen that the string is hidden behind the left forefinger, which looks very natural holding the straw in two pieces.

7. The view from your side is almost as convincing! Begin to pull one end of the string downwards.

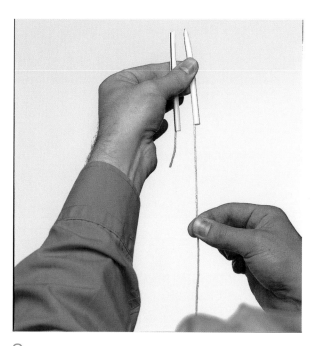

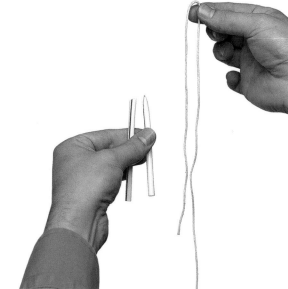

8. Continue pulling until the string is removed completely. Pause to let the effect register with your audience.

9. Show that the string is completely restored. If you wish, you can immediately hand the string out for examination, but be sure to discard the straw in case the slit is discovered.

jumping rubber band

A rubber band is placed over the first and second fingers, and then magically caused to jump to the third and fourth fingers. This is a very simple trick that you will have no trouble mastering.

1. Place a rubber band over the first and second fingers. The back of your hand should be towards the audience. Pull the band away from your hand.

Secret View

2. Close your hand, inserting all the fingers into the rubber band. Let the band snap over the fingertips. From the front, it will simply look as though the band is on the first and second fingers.

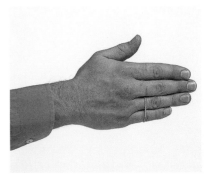

3. Quickly open your hand. The band will automatically jump over to the third and fourth fingers.

Secret View

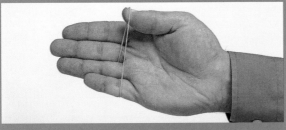

4. It is possible to make the band jump back again. The move can also be accomplished with one hand. Hook your thumb under the band and stretch it up so that you create a gap, as before.

Secret View

5. Close the fingers again, inserting them into the gap created. Release your thumb from the band.

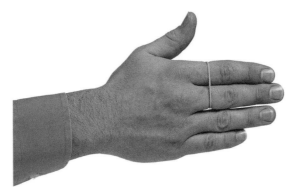

6. Open the hand again, and the band will jump back to its former position.

string through arm (version 1)

A piece of string is tied into a continuous loop. It is wrapped around a spectator's arm and magically penetrates the flesh and bone without any damage whatsoever! The principle relies on your moves being quick and smooth. The secret move is covered by the speed of the hand, which in this case really does deceive the eye. A piece of string is a simple, compact prop to carry around.

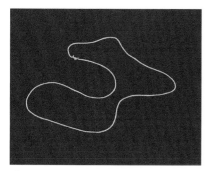

1. Tie a piece of string, approximately 3 ft (90 cm) long, into a loop with a strong knot.

2. Hold the loop under a spectator's arm and ask her to create an impenetrable barrier by gripping her hands firmly together, as seen here.

3. Bring both ends of the string up to meet each other, and then pass one loop through the other. Grip the string and tug it gently to show that it is unquestionably trapped on the arm.

4. Move both hands up to each other again, and then hook the left first finger around the top strand of the right hand's string.

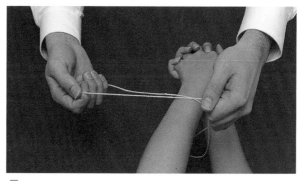

5. Maintain the first finger's grip, but release the other portion of string from the left hand.

6. Pull both hands apart until the string is held taut. It will now be above the spectator's arm. It is important that steps 4, 5 and 6 happen together in one smooth motion in order for the illusion to look its best.

string through arm (version 2)

A spectator holds out his arm and a piece of string is held underneath. A few tugs and the string passes straight through his arm to the other side! Or does it?

To prepare for this trick you need to thread two small beads on a piece of string, approximately 18 in (45 cm) long, tying a knot at each end. The beads should be loose and free to slide from one end to the other. These beads are not meant to be a secret, but neither should you call attention to them. When you pinch your finger and thumb around them, you should hardly be able to see them. Try to ensure that the knots at the ends of the string are tied as tightly as possible so that they do not come undone while performing.

1. Starting with both beads at the left end of the string, place the string under the outstretched arm of a spectator. The string should be held taut and at the fingertips.

2. Bring both ends of the string together. Grip one of the beads tightly with your right fingers, keeping the end bead gripped in your left hand.

3. Allow the end of the string held by the right hand to drop, and then quickly pull both beads taut. What really happens is that the string passes under the arm.

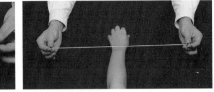

4. At full speed, the eye cannot detect the route the string takes. The illusion of the string passing through the arm to get to the other side is very convincing!

string through ring

You can make a piece of string pass through many other solid objects. Here the same trick is performed using a spectator's finger ring.

As before, you need to attach two small beads to a piece of string. Then ask a spectator to lend you a ring. The best type of ring to use is a plain wedding band. In any event, you should avoid borrowing rings that have precious stones, in case one of them should fall out.

1. Ask a spectator to pinch a ring tightly between his finger and thumb. Thread the string through the ring. Both beads must be to the left.

2. Bring both hands together, pinching a bead between finger and thumb of each hand.

3. Drop the end held in your right hand and pull the beads apart.

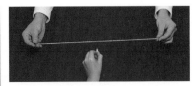

4. The string appears to have melted through the band of metal. A little thought will reveal many other objects that could be used instead of a spectator's arm or a finger ring – the handle of a mug, for example.

rope through neck

The two ends of a piece of rope are seen hanging over both shoulders. Despite the fact that the rope clearly passes around the back of the head, with a sharp tug it visibly penetrates the neck. This trick also works very well with a tie, which is perhaps a more appropriate item to have hanging around your neck! Please note that care should be taken when wrapping any sort of cord around your neck.

1. To prepare, run the rope across the front of your neck, and tuck it just under the edge of your shirt collar.

2. Once this secret preparation has been accomplished, you are ready to perform. Viewed from the front, it looks as if you have a piece of rope hanging around your neck and over your shoulders.

3. Hold both ends of the rope and pull gently until the line becomes taut.

4. With one quick action, pull the rope hard with both hands. As the rope stretches out, it is pulled from under your collar so quickly that the eye will be unable to detect the secret.

rope through neck again!

The general rule is "Never repeat a trick," but there are exceptions, for example, when you have several methods for achieving the same effect. This is the ideal follow-up to Rope through Neck because the method is completely different, even though the two tricks look very similar. Once again, a tie will work just as well, and as mentioned before you should take care whenever looping cord around your neck.

1. Hang a piece of rope, approximately 6 ft (1.8 m) long, around your neck so that the left side hangs lower than the right. Experimentation will make it clear exactly how much rope should be hanging from either side.

2. With the right hand, grasp the left side of the rope between your thumb and first finger about a quarter of the way down. Now reach over with the left hand and pinch the right side of the rope about a quarter of the way up from the bottom.

3. Lift the right hand, with the rope, across the front of your neck and around to the middle of the back of your neck.

4. A split second after the right hand has started moving, the left hand begins its journey. It takes its piece of rope and wraps it around the back of your neck from right to left (the same way as the first piece). Your left arm moves over your head to achieve this.

Secret View

5. The result is a bight, or loop of rope, which is held by the loop made by the shorter piece.

6. From the front, it looks as if you have wrapped the rope around your neck. Hold one end in each hand and pull the rope taut.

7. Pull sharply with both hands. The bight of rope will slip out of the other loop, and the rope will fall away from your neck. Make sure the rope is pulled completely taut.

hunter bow knot

In this trick, a slip knot is tied into a length of rope with a pretty flourish. This method of tying a slip knot is quite tricky to learn, but once you understand the moves, you will never forget them.

The beauty of this particular tie is that the knots created look completely tangled until they all dissolve into thin air! You can incorporate the Hunter Bow Knot into other rope tricks and routines.

1. Extend the first and second fingers of your left hand, and hang the center of a piece of rope over them. Position your right first and second fingers about 1–2 in (2.5–5 cm) down the rope, below the left second finger.

2. Move the right hand back, under and up, curling your fingers enough to pull the rope back, and loop it around the tips of your left fingers.

3. With both hands, grip a portion of the rope between your first and second fingers, as shown here.

4. Gripping tightly, pull the right hand to the right and the left hand to the left. The result will be a bow.

5. Reach into the tops of both loops and pull the ends through.

6. Slowly pull both ends of the rope, tightening the knot.

7. Give one final tug, and the knot will disappear! If you find that the knot does not dissolve, you may need to experiment at step 5 by pulling the ends of the rope through the opposite sides of the loops.

impossible knot

Challenge a spectator to tie a knot in the center of a piece of rope without letting go of the ends. Although you may find this difficult to learn initially, once you understand which hand goes where you will be able to make the Impossible Knot in an instant, without thinking.

1. Hold one end of a piece of rope tightly in each hand.

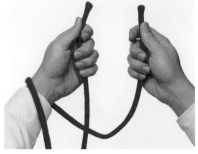

2. Loop the right hand over your left arm and behind the rope held in your left hand. Bring it back to a position similar to that at the start. Now move your right hand through the loop marked "X."

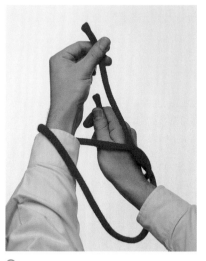

3. Once your hand has passed through the loop, pass it through the second loop marked "X."

4. Stretch both hands out. You should now be in this position.

5. Allow the rope to slip off your left wrist, and then pull the rope taut.

6. Repeat this with the right loop. You will be left with a knot in the center of the rope.

7. Tug both ends, and the knot will disappear before your eyes!

slip knot

A knot is tied without letting go of the ends of the rope. The knot is then plucked off the rope and thrown into the audience! This is a great "bit of business" to add to a longer rope routine because it always receives a laugh from the audience.

Secret View

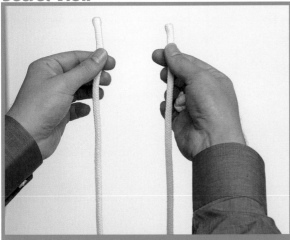

1. You will need a length of rope and a knot cut from a spare piece of rope. To prepare, hide the extra knot in your right-hand finger palm position. Hold one end of the main piece of rope in each hand.

2. Tie a knot without letting go of the ends of the rope, as described in Impossible Knot. Hold one end of the rope in the left hand.

Secret View

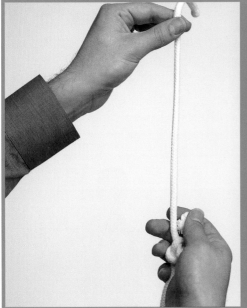

3. With the right hand, approach the knot in the rope, and with the little finger, grip the rope just under the knot. The fourth finger tugs the rope, undoing the knot as you simultaneously pluck the knot off the rope, bringing the hidden knot into view in the fingertips.

4. Viewed from the front, the illusion looks very convincing. Finish by tossing the knot high into the air and into the audience.

cut and restored rope (version 1)

A length of rope is unmistakably cut in half, yet it is magically restored to its former condition. This is an absolute classic of magic and is still performed today by many magicians. You can follow this version with the next. They work perfectly together.

1. To prepare, place a pair of scissors in your right pocket. Bend a short piece of rope, approximately 4 in (10 cm) long, in half and hold it secretly in the left hand between the thumb and first finger. This piece must remain hidden at all times.

Secret View

2. To begin your performance, hold a longer piece of rope, approximately 6 ft (1.8 m) long, next to the short piece, as shown. From the front, it looks as though you have only one piece of rope.

Secret View

3. With the right hand, grab the center of the rope and bring it up to the hidden short piece. It will look as though you are simply repositioning the middle of the rope so that it can be displayed. In reality, you are going to switch the ropes.

Secret View

4. Clip the "real" center between your left thumb and first finger while extending the short piece up into view. The move should take seconds and should arouse no suspicion.

5. Remove the scissors from your pocket. From the front, the image is very clear. You have simply found the center of a piece of rope and are holding it before cutting it in half.

6. Cleanly cut the rope in half. Of course you are actually cutting through the center of the short piece.

7. Trim the ends of the rope, allowing the pieces to drop onto the floor. Continue trimming until all of the short piece of rope has been cut and dropped so that you destroy the evidence in front of the audience! Make a magical gesture, and then stretch out the rope between both hands to show that it is completely restored.

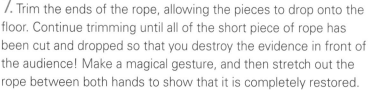

cut and restored rope (version 2)

This version of this famous trick follows very well after the first. Try it out and you will fool yourself! As you will see, with the extra knot in your right hand, you can follow this with the Slip Knot trick. This illusion works because it becomes difficult to follow exactly which section of the rope is being cut. While it looks like the center, it is actually a piece just a very short distance from one of the ends.

1. Hold the center of a piece of rope, approximately 5–6 ft (1.5–1.8 m) long, with your left hand and bring the right end of the rope up to meet it. With your left thumb and fingers, grip the rope about 3 in (7.5 cm) from the end.

2. Loop the short end of the rope away from you and over the top of the center. Bring it back underneath, as shown. Thread the end through the gap marked "X."

3. Pull the short end of the rope and the part that emerges below the knot, to tighten the knot.

4. Cut the left-hand side of the loop just under the knot.

5. Clearly display what looks like a piece of rope cut in two and held together with a knot. Actually the rope is in one piece and the knot is simply a tiny section of rope tied around the center.

Secret View

6. Begin to wind the rope around the fingers of your left hand. As you reach the knot, allow it to slip along, hidden in the fingers of your right hand.

Secret View

7. Continue to wind the rope until the knot falls off the end. Keep the knot hidden in the finger palm position.

8. Stretch out the rope between both hands to show that it has restored itself. You are now in a perfect position to continue with another rope trick of your choice.

rope through apple

An apple is cored and two long pieces of rope are threaded through. To further secure the apple to the ropes, a knot is made. Despite the impossibility of the situation, the apple is pulled free of the ropes without any harm to either.

This routine is ideal for a large crowd as well as a more intimate gathering. Although only small props are used, they can be made to fill a large stage with a spectator on either side of you. It is an effect that, as magic advertisements would say, "Packs Flat, Plays Big."

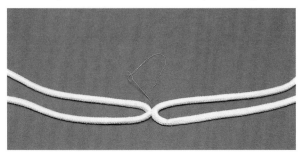

1. Prepare two pieces of rope, each about 6 ft (1.8 m) long, by folding them in half. Loosely stitch the centers together. The stitches should not be too tight because they must be snapped at a later stage.

2. In performance, unfold the ropes so that they run parallel to each other. Invite two people to help you, and give them two ends each. Ask them to tug on the ropes to prove that they are exactly what they appear to be.

Secret View

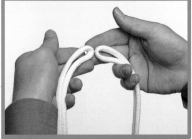

3. Hold on to the center of the ropes, and ask your helpers to let go. As the ends drop, grip the center of the ropes with both hands, and switch one of the ropes around, arranging them so that they are held together by the stitches. The thread is hidden from the front by your fingers, and the repositioning happens as you raise the ropes to temporarily place them over your shoulders.

4. With the ropes now safely resting around your shoulders, your hands are free to pick up an apple corer and remove the core from the apple.

5. Remove the rope from around your neck, hiding the center in your left hand. Thread the ends of the ropes through the apple. (The two ends that go into the apple belong to the same piece of rope.)

Secret View

6. The left hand provides enough cover to prevent the center section of the rope being seen. Continue to pull the ropes through the apple until the joint is hidden inside it.

7. Ask the spectators to hold the ends of the ropes. To secure the apple further, suggest tying a knot in the ropes. Take one end from each side (it doesn't matter which), and tie a simple overhand knot. Give the ends back to the spectators.

8. Cover the apple with a handkerchief, explaining that the magic has to happen under the cover of darkness!

9. Reach underneath and ask the spectators to pull the ropes taut. The thread will snap, and the ropes will automatically fall away from the apple. You may find it helpful to slide the apple back and forth along the ropes as they are pulled taut.

10. Display the apple, and remove the handkerchief. Give the apple to one spectator and the ropes to the other to be examined. The secret to the trick was destroyed by the spectators themselves!

coin under bottle caps

A coin is placed under one of three bottle tops. The caps are rearranged while your back is turned, yet you find the coin immediately. The method to this trick relies on a short length of thread or hair which remains unseen by the spectators. Experiment with different surfaces to work on. A tablecloth with a busy design would be perfect.

1.Fabric shops sell a thread that is almost invisible to the human eye. You will need to find some of this "invisible thread" or use a substitute such as a hair. Attach a small piece of this thread or hair to the underside of a coin with a piece of adhesive tape. (White thread is used here for ease of explanation.)

2. It is a good idea to have this coin among others in your pocket and to casually bring it out, putting the others away. Make sure that the taped side of the coin is against the table. Place three bottle caps on the table, and ask a spectator to choose any one of them to cover the coin.

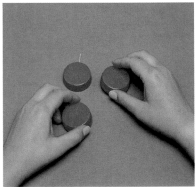

3. Ask the spectator to slide the bottle caps around while your back is turned. Explain that when you turn back you will try to divine which bottle cap the coin is under.

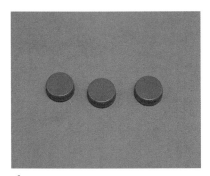

4.When she has finished mixing the bottle caps, turn around and casually glance down in order to spot the thread. Try not to make this glance too obvious.

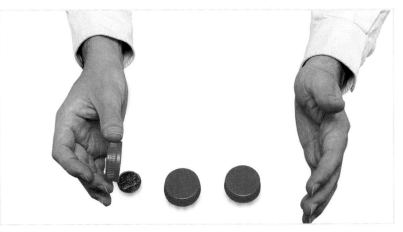

5.Act as though you are receiving psychic vibes, perhaps hovering your hands just above each bottle cap in order to feel the heat rising from the coin. After suitable byplay, lift the appropriate bottle cap to reveal the coin.

whispering jack

Any five cards are removed from the deck and placed facedown on the table. A spectator looks at and remembers one. The five cards are then mixed and are again placed facedown on the table. Despite the fact that even the spectator is now unsure where his card is, the magician is able to find the one selected. Whispering Jack is a great trick to perform with a borrowed deck because the owner will know that the cards could not be marked in any way and therefore will be even more baffled. You can use any number of cards for this trick, but five seems about right. Once you read the method, you will realize that the older the deck of cards, the easier this trick is to perform.

1. Remove a jack from a deck of old cards. Explain that this card represents Sherlock Holmes, the world-famous detective. Ask a spectator to remove any other five cards from the deck and to lay them facedown in a row on the table.

4. Your real reason for doing this is to create "misdirection" while you carefully look at the back of the chosen card in order to find a mark, blemish or piece of dirt that you will be able to recognize later. Study the cards secretively and quickly; otherwise, someone may see you staring at them.

2. Ask the spectator to pick up any of the five cards, remember it and then replace it. This card represents the villain. Although you do not see the face of the chosen card, you must see which position the card is taken from.

5. Ask the spectator to mix the cards until even he cannot know where his card is. Ask him to lay out the cards on the table as before.

3. Explain that the detective must interview each of the suspects. As you say this, tap each card with the corner of the jack.

6. Explain that Sherlock Holmes will now interview each suspect again and find the villain. Tap the corner of the jack onto the back of every card as before while you secretly look for the mark you spotted earlier.

7. Turn over the card – the great detective has found his man!

"X" marks the spot

A deck of cards is placed on the table in full view. It is explained that one of the cards has been marked and the spectator has to guess which one. A card is named—it can be any card at all. This card is removed from the deck and is shown to be the only one marked with a large "X." This is a superb card trick. It will only take a few minutes to prepare and a little practice to learn.

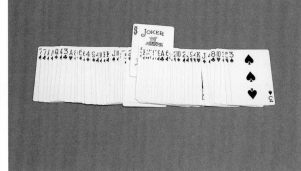

1 Prepare the cards by dividing the deck into two packets of 26 cards. Mark one packet with an "X" on the front of every card and the other packet with an "X" on the back of every card. While the "X" should be bold and clear, it should not fill the entire card, and it must be positioned in the center.

2 Arrange these cards so that (from the top down) you have the front-marked cards followed by the back-marked cards, with a joker dividing the two packets. Square up the deck and place it back inside the card box.

3 In performance, say "Before the show I marked one of these cards with an 'X.' I am going to try to influence your decision and make you think of the card of my choice. The only clue I will give you is that it is not the joker! Name any card in the deck." There are two possibilities. The first is that the chosen card will have an "X" on the back. Let us deal with this situation first. Remove the deck from the box and spread the cards faceup to find the chosen card. Do not spread the cards too wide because after the center point of the deck you will risk exposing the Xs. Find the chosen card (in our example, the Four of Hearts). Remove the card, keeping it faceup. Spread through the first half of the deck faceup, explaining that any card could have been named.

4. Turn the deck facedown, and display the top half of the deck in a spread or fan, subtly showing the backs of these cards. Again, do not spread too far down the deck.

5. Keep the top few cards spread wide as you reveal that the back of the chosen card has an "X" printed on it.

6. The second possibility is that the chosen card has an "X" on the front. Again, carefully spread through the cards until you find the one selected. The spread must be tight. Begin to pull out the card.

7. Before the "X" is revealed, turn the fan facedown. Deal the chosen card facedown on to the table.

8. Casually spread the top quarter or so of the cards, displaying the backs, and turn the deck faceup. Spread them widely, explaining that any card could have been chosen.

9. Turn the selected card faceup to display the "X." The great thing about this trick is that the spectators are convinced that they saw the backs and fronts of all the cards.

dice divination

While the magician's back is turned, two dice are rolled a number of times and the numbers totalled. When the magician turns around, he or she is instantly able to reveal the total.

It is a little-known fact that the two numbers on the opposite side of any die always add up to 7. Using this principle, you can gain the knowledge you need to discern the total.

1. Turn your back to a spectator and ask him to follow your instructions carefully. Ask him to roll a pair of dice, and add both numbers together.
In our example it is 6 + 1 = 7.

2. Ask him to pick up one of the dice and add its bottom number to the total (7 + 6 = 13).

3. Tell him to roll the first die again and add the number that lands uppermost (4 + 13 = 17). Turn back and glance at both dice. Simply add 7 to whatever numbers you see facing up. In our example, 6 + 4 + 7 = 17.

human calculator

Six-digit numbers are selected by the spectator and the magician. Impossible as it may sound, the final total is found to have been predicted in advance. This is a very clever mathematical trick. As you will see, the simple formula of subtracting and adding 2 does all the work for you. The great thing about the Human Calculator is that you finish with a different number every time.

1. Give a piece of paper and a pen to a spectator and ask him to openly write down any six-figure number. Let us assume it is 2 1 7 3 4 9. You base your prediction on this number. Simply deduct 2 from the last digit and add 2 in front of the first digit. In our example, you would write down 2 2 1 7 3 4 7. Place this prediction to one side, out of view. This is written while you ask the spectator to write another six figure-number underneath the first. As soon as he starts writing, jot down your prediction.

2. Let us assume his two numbers are:
2 1 7 3 4 9
6 1 3 9 4 8
Now you write a six-digit number underneath. Each number you write must total 9 when added to the number above.
So you would write:
2 1 7 3 4 9
6 1 3 9 4 8
3 8 6 0 5 1
Ask the spectator to write another number below yours:
2 1 7 3 4 9
6 1 3 9 4 8
3 8 6 0 5 1
1 2 9 3 0 6

Finally, you write one last number in exactly the same way as before:
2 1 7 3 4 9
6 1 3 9 4 8
3 8 6 0 5 1
1 2 9 3 0 6
8 7 0 6 9 3

3. Give the spectator a calculator and ask him to work out the total:
2217347
You can now reveal that your prediction matches the total. (If the last digit in the first number is either 0 or 1, subtract 2 from the last two digits, that is, 3 5 7 8 3 0 would give you a prediction of 2 3 5 7 8 2 8.)

impossible prediction

Three cards are displayed, and a spectator is asked to choose one of them. It is a completely free choice, and the spectator can change her mind as many times as she wishes. The magician reveals a prediction that has been in view throughout, which matches her choice. The method to this trick relies on a principle known as a "multiple out." All three possible outcomes can be displayed as three separate predictions, but the audience is only ever aware of one of them, so the prediction seems impossible. You cannot repeat this particular trick to the same audience twice, but it is one of the most baffling tricks you will ever perform.

1. To prepare the three predictions, draw a large "X" on the back of a picture card. Photocopy two other cards, reducing the size, and then cut them out. Glue one of the mini photocopies on the flap side of an envelope. Keep the other photocopy loose.

2. Place all three cards, faceup, inside the envelope together with the loose photocopy. With this envelope in your pocket, you will always be ready to show a miracle.

3. Casually introduce the envelope and explain that you have three cards inside. The photocopy glued to the back must remain hidden. Remove the cards, taking care that the loose photocopy does not fall out, and lay them out, faceup, keeping the "X" hidden. Place the envelope to one side, but in the spectator's field of vision. Ask them to choose one of the cards.

4. Give the spectator the opportunity to change her mind. There are three possible outcomes. First, let us assume the picture card is chosen. Explain that before the performance you marked the back of just one of the cards with an "X." Slowly turn over the cards one by one to reveal the "X" on the back of the selected card.

5. In this example, the second scenario would be the Five of Spades. Explain that you gave the spectator every opportunity to change her mind and that this is the card you were sure she would choose. Slowly turn the envelope over to show your prediction pasted on the back.

6. The final scenario is that the Three of Clubs is chosen. Once again explain that you had a prediction, which has been in full view the entire time. Slowly tip up the envelope so that the loose photocopy falls from within the envelope. It matches the selection.

four card poker

While the magician's back is turned, two dice are rolled a number of times and the numbers totalled. When the magician turns around they are instantly able to reveal the total. It is a little-known fact that the two numbers on the opposite side of any die always add up to 7. Using this principle, you can gain the knowledge you need to discern the total.

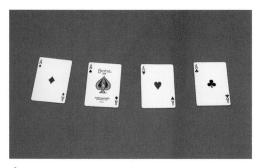

1. Set the four aces out onto the table next to each other.

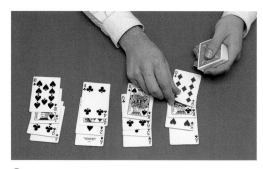

2. Deal three cards on top of each ace. Place the rest of the deck to one side.

3. Collect each pile, one on top of the other, into one packet. Turn the cards facedown and square them neatly.

4. Cut the cards several times, each time ensuring that it is a complete cut. Cutting will not mix the order of the cards; it will merely change the cyclical order. You can even let a spectator do the cutting, which seems to increase the impossibility of any sleight of hand.

5. Re-deal the cards into four piles, side by side. As long as the cards have only been cut and not shuffled, the four aces will automatically be dealt together in one pile.

6. Square each pile, secretly "glimpsing" the bottom card each time. You must discover which pile the aces are in, but do so without making your glimpse obvious.

7. There are now several possible outcomes to this trick. Ask a spectator to point to a pile with one hand. If he points to the pile of aces, simply turn over that pile and show that, despite a completely free choice, he has found all four aces.

8. If he points to a different pile, ask him to point to another packet with his other hand. If both piles picked do not contain the aces, remove them, explaining that they are to be discarded. This will leave you with two piles. If, however, the second pile pointed to does contain the aces, remove the other two piles, leaving two piles on the table.

9. Either way, one of the remaining piles will consist of the four aces. Explain that you are going to play a very simple game of Four Card Poker and that the spectator must choose a hand for you and a hand for himself. Ask the spectator to push one pile of cards towards you. Give him an opportunity to change his mind.

10. If the aces are pushed towards you, turn both packets faceup and display them. Explain that even though he had every chance to change his mind, he gave you the winning hand! If the aces are kept by the spectator, simply show your cards and ask to see his, exclaiming that he is extremely lucky and that you would not want to play cards with him! If you are not 100 percent confident with the three possible outcomes of this trick, your audience may be confused as to what was supposed to have happened. Practice until you can perform this without thinking about what to do next.

tri-thought

Three spectators are asked to make a choice. One chooses a number between 1 and 100, the second chooses a shape and the third chooses a card. The magician has predicted all three choices. Tri-Thought uses the "one-ahead" principle. As its name suggests, you are always one step ahead of your audience, which is how you are able to predict their choices. This routine will baffle people completely if performed with confidence and boldness. It does require you to perform well, and it is not a trick for someone with a nervous disposition!

1. The "one-ahead" principle requires you to know what the final choice will be. This is why you use a deck of cards. You must know what card is on top of the deck before you begin. In our example, it is the Ten of Clubs.

2. Ask a spectator to think of a number between 1 and 100. Pretend you are reading his mind and explain that you are writing down a prediction. What you actually write on the paper is the card that was at the top of the deck (the Ten of Clubs). Fold up the paper into quarters and explain that it represents prediction number "1." However, instead of writing "1" on the folded paper, secretly write "3."

3. Drop this piece of paper into a mug so that it is temporarily out of sight. It is vital that the spectators do not see that you have incorrectly numbered the paper. The mug also prevents anyone from being able to keep track of which paper is which.

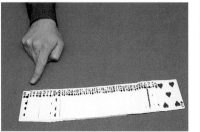

4. Ask the spectator to confirm the number he was thinking of. Let us assume he says "43." Act as though you knew all along "43" was his number and say "That's uncanny, let's try to get two out of two." Ask another spectator to think of a shape, and once again pretend to read her mind as you write a second prediction. What you actually write is the number you just heard: "43." Fold this paper into quarters and write "1" on it, but say that it is your second prediction.

5. Drop the second paper into the mug. Ask the spectator to confirm her chosen shape. Let us assume she says "Square." Once again, act smug and say you will try one more prediction.

6. Now force the card, using any force method you are comfortable with. Shown here is a slip force. Begin by riffling down the edge of the deck until a spectator stops you. Then cut the deck at this point, slipping the top card to the chosen position.

7. Offer the forced card to the spectator, but ask him not to look at it for the moment and to place it facedown, off to one side.

8. Write your final prediction, but instead of writing the name of a card, write or draw the shape mentioned in step 5 – in this case, a square. Fold the paper into quarters and write "2" on it as you explain to your audience that this is the third and final prediction.

9. Drop the paper into the mug with the other predictions. Using the one-ahead principle, you have made three predictions that now match the three choices of the spectators.

10. Ask the spectator to reveal the chosen card. It will be the card you wrote at the start. Act pleased with yourself again, and tip the papers out onto the table, arranging them in numerical order.

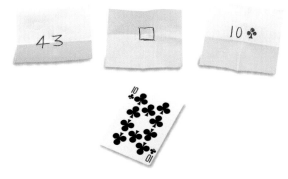

11. Open your predictions one by one, showing your perfect mind-reading capabilities!

face value

The magician removes a card from the deck and places it to one side as a prediction for later on. A random number of cards are dealt onto the table by a spectator, and two piles are made. The top card of each pile is turned over, and the suit of one together with the value of another are combined and found to match the earlier prediction. This is a simple but very baffling card trick.

1. Ask a spectator to shuffle the cards and then hand the deck to you. Fan the cards towards yourself and take note of the top two cards – simply remember the value of the first card and the suit of the second. This combined card will become your prediction. In our example, the prediction would be the Four of Clubs. Remove it and place it to one side, but in full view.

2. Give the deck back to the spectator, and ask her to deal the cards onto a table, one on top of the other until she wishes to stop dealing. The original top two cards of the deck are now at the bottom of this pile. In order to get them to the top again, the cards must be dealt once more.

3. Discard the rest of the deck, and have the pile of cards on the table dealt alternately into two piles. Notice which pile the final card is placed on.

4. Turn over whichever card was dealt last, explaining that you will use the card's value only and ignore the suit. (In our example it is the Four of Hearts.)

5. Turn over the top card of the other pile and explain that you will use the suit, but not the value (the Two of Clubs).

6. Reveal that your earlier prediction matches the combination of the cards randomly shuffled to the top of the two piles.

tip On a rare occasion you may find that the first two cards of the deck will not produce a usable prediction. For example, if the Six of Clubs were next to the Six of Spades the prediction should be the Six of Spades, but that card cannot be removed from the deck. If this happens, cut the deck, positioning two new cards at the top. Unless you are very unlucky, these new top cards should be usable.

you find it!

The deck is given to a spectator – the magician never touches it throughout the trick. A card is chosen and returned to the deck, which is then cut a number of times. The magician merely glances at the side of the deck and tells the spectator the exact position of the selected card.

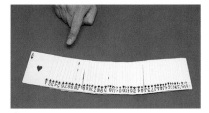

1. To set up the deck, sort all the hearts into numerical order, ace through king. Place this stack on the bottom of the deck, with the ace lowermost.

2. Set the deck facedown in front of a spectator and instruct him to cut off half the cards.

3. Ask him to look at the card he cut to and to remember it.

4. Have the card replaced on the opposite pile (on top of the original top card).

5. Instruct him to complete the cut and square the cards neatly.

6. Now ask him to turn the deck faceup.

7. Instruct the spectator to cut and complete the cut. What you need him to do is to cut to one of the cards in the stack that you set up earlier (that is, any heart). If you are lucky, he will do this the first time; if not, simply ask him to cut the deck again, and again if necessary. Eventually he will cut somewhere into the stack of hearts. In our example, it is the Four of Hearts. Just remember "four."

8. Have the deck turned facedown, and stare at the edge of the deck as if making some difficult calculations. State that his selection is "four" cards down from the top of the deck. After all the cutting, this seems quite a bold statement to make – even the spectator has lost track of the card. Ask him to deal three cards facedown and turn over the fourth. It will be the card selected.

tip A Jack counts as 11, a Queen as 12 and a King as 13.

1089

A number is chosen at random and is shown to match an earlier prediction. This is an interesting mathematical principle with many uses. The number will always be 1089.

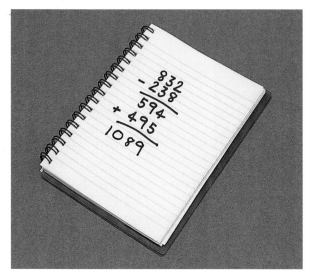

1. Ask somebody to write down any three-figure number, for example:

        8 3 2

Ask her to reverse the number and to subtract the smaller number from the larger:

        8 3 2
    -   2 3 8
        5 9 4

Now ask her to reverse the total and to add both numbers together:

        8 3 2
    -   2 3 8
        5 9 4
    +   4 9 5
        1 0 8 9

2. Try this with various numbers. It is possible that when you reach the final stage the spectator only has a three-digit number. If so, the number will always be 198. Ask how many digits are in her final number. If she says "Three," simply add another step. Ask her to reverse her total once again and to

add the numbers together again. This will ensure the total is 1089.

Because the number is always the same, you cannot repeat this trick to the same audience. However, you can take advantage of this knowledge, as follows.

1089 – book test

Here the distraction of the book is a smoke screen, a layer of "misdirection" designed to take the audience's attention away from the true method, which is clearly mathematical.

1. To prepare, take a book and look up page 10. Go down eight lines and look at the ninth word. Write this word on a piece of paper and seal it in an envelope.

2. At the beginning of your performance, introduce the sealed envelope containing your prediction, and ask a spectator to look after it.

3. Perform 1089 as detailed above, but do not ask the spectator to reveal the total out loud. Show your book and ask that the first two digits be used to find a page. Ask the spectator to turn to that page (page 10). The next digit, you explain, is to represent a line on that page and the final digit is to represent a word on that line. Once the word has been found, ask the spectator to read it out loud. Take back the book and have the envelope opened to show that your prediction matches the chosen word.

tip For an extra subtlety, choose a book in which the eighth line down on page 10 does not exist. When your spectator tells you there isn't a word there, ask her to turn to the next page instead. This little hiccup makes it seem unlikely that you knew which page was going to be chosen.

double book test

A book is chosen from a stack of books and a page and line are chosen completely at random. The magician leaves the room so it is impossible to cheat. From the chosen line, one word is decided on. The book is closed. The magician comes back into the room and, using the hidden powers of the human mind, is able to write down the word being thought of.

1. You can use as many books as you wish, but for every book you must have a duplicate copy hidden in another room. Ask a spectator to choose one of the books and note the title. Ask for a random page number to be called out, and also a line number. Then ask for a small number between 1 and 10, to indicate the word on the line. Explain that to avoid any cheating, you will leave the room until the book

has been looked at. Once the door is closed, simply look up the corresponding page, line and word in the duplicate book.

2. When you re-enter the room, act like a mind reader and theatrically reveal the chosen word – you could write it down on a large sheet of paper and ask the spectator to shout out the word first before you show your prediction.

tip It is also possible to do this trick while remaining in the same room. You will need a friend at the back of the room. He or she looks up the word for you and writes it down on a large sheet and holds it up so that you can see it. Everyone else is looking at you, so they will not look behind them.

the big prediction

A large prediction is shown to the audience and displayed in full view. Then a card is chosen from a shuffled deck. The prediction is shown and, after some comical byplay, is proved to be correct. This effect is best for a large audience. It shows how a simple idea can be made to work for a big crowd using few props – a classic example of "Packs Flat, Plays Big." If you begin in a very serious manner, the moment of comedy – when the cards are seen stuck to the back of the board – can be very funny.

1. To prepare, make a prediction by folding a poster board in half. On one of the outer sides draw a large question mark. On the other, glue one set of cards in four rows. The cards should be in suit and numerical order, and each index should be visible.

2. The inside of the board should be made to resemble a giant playing card (in this example, the Ace of Clubs). Use a computer to generate the image; then cut and paste it onto the board.

3. Take another deck of cards and place a duplicate of the prediction on the bottom of the deck, in preparation to force this card on a spectator.

4. Force this card, using any force method you are confident with.

5. In performance, show the prediction (with the question mark towards the audience) and place it to one side. Take the deck of cards and give them a quick shuffle, making sure the force card remains in the appropriate position. Force the Ace of Clubs, and then give the spectator the cards to shuffle and mix. You no longer need the cards anyway.

6. Once again, show the prediction and ask the audience if they would be impressed if the chosen card was on the other side of the board. Turn over the board and show the complete deck. Appear to search for a few seconds, then point out the selected card.

7. After the laughter subsides, open the board completely to show that your prediction really does match the chosen card. Try this out the next time you get a chance to perform for a large group of people. It is a good example of how the presentation is sometimes more important than the trick itself, which in this case is fairly basic.

black magic

This is one of the few tricks for which you need a "stooge" or assistant, someone you can trust to keep the secret. The stooge is asked to leave the room (out of earshot) while a member of the audience names any object in sight. The stooge returns and the magician explains that, using the power of the human mind, he will send his thoughts across the room so that this person will be able to reveal which object was chosen. The magician points at various objects in the room – maybe ten in total – and the stooge is indeed able to choose the correct object.

You can repeat this trick without fear of the secret being found out if each time you change the objects and the number of things you point to.

method The secret to Black Magic is in the title! As with many tricks, the method is very simple. Simply tell your assistant beforehand that you will point to a number of items. One of them will be black. The next object will be the chosen object. This is a very adaptable trick because you can use absolutely anything, anywhere. The stooge should act as if trying to read your mind.

Left: A number of objects, which can easily be found on a desk in an office, could be used for this trick – for example, a stapler, scissors, envelope, pen, cup and adhesive tape.

temple of wisdom

The magician explains that mind reading requires someone to act as the sender and another to act as the receiver. A spectator is chosen to act as the receiver and leaves the room. While she is out of the room, the rest of the audience decides on a small number. Let us assume it is 12. The participant comes back into the room and places her fingertips on the temples of the magician (the sender), who pretends to send the number psychically. The receiver concentrates hard and then correctly reveals the chosen number. This can be repeated as many times as you wish.

The method relies on a "stooge" whom you have briefed before the performance and whom you can trust to keep the secret. This trick can be repeated as many times as you wish.

method When the stooge touches your temples, pass on the chosen number by the subtle action of clenching your jaw. Your temples will pulse each time you squeeze, without anybody else noticing. Try thinking of other ways to signal the number such as the position of your feet or the number of fingers you are holding open in your lap. These subtle codes can be very baffling and are great party tricks.

GLOSSARY

book test A classic effect of mental magic in which a spectator selects a letter, word, sentence or illustration in a book, and the magician divines or predicts it.

byplay Secondary activity performed by the magician for dramatic effect.

cut and restored An effect in which a magician cuts something into pieces and then makes it whole again.

effect The intended and perceived result of a magic trick.

force The action of controlling a spectator's choice while making the spectator believe that the choice was free and fair.

illusion A magical effect that looks impossible to spectators but is accomplished through real-world means.

impromptu Performed on the spot without any special preparation.

matrix A magic routine in which four small objects are placed apart and covered (usually by cards or the magician's hands), and the objects magically assemble, one by one, in a single place.

method The secret workings of a trick; the technique a magician uses to achieve the desired effect.

misdirection The skill of focusing the audience's attention elsewhere while performing a secret move.

one-ahead principle A principle in which the magician uses previously obtained information to stay one step ahead of the audience and make amazingly accurate predictions.

palming The act of secretly hiding an object in the hand. There are several different palms in magic (classic palm, finger palm, back palm, etc.), not all of which use the palm of the hand itself.

patter The dialogue a magician uses to accompany a trick or routine.

psychic Capable of extraordinary mental processes, such as extrasensory perception.

repertoire The entire stock of skills, techniques or devices used by a performer.

sleight of hand A type of magic that requires skill and quickness in manipulating objects with the hands.

spectator A single member of the audience.

stooge A secret accomplice in the audience who helps make the magic happen.

Genii Magazine
4200 Wisconsin Avenue NW, Suite 106-384
Washington, DC 20016
(301) 652-5800
Web site: http://geniimagazine.com
Founded in 1936, *Genii, The Conjurers' Magazine* is the oldest American magazine for magicians. The periodical appears monthly in both print and digital formats with over one hundred pages of articles, magic tricks, reviews and more.

International Brotherhood of Magicians (IBM)
13 Point West Boulevard
St. Charles, MO 63301-4431
(636) 724-2400
Web site: http://www.magician.org
The International Brotherhood of Magicians (IBM) is a well-respected magic organization with about three hundred "rings," or branches, worldwide. The volunteer-led group welcomes anyone with an interest in the art of magic. There are programs and resources designed especially for youth members.

Magicana
17 Madison Avenue
Toronto, ON M5R 2S2
Canada
(416) 913-9034
Web site: http://www.magicana.com
Magicana is an organization dedicated to exploring and advancing magic as a performing art. Its activities include performances by leading magicians, exhibitions, workshops and seminars, and publications. Its outreach programs for children and seniors employ magic as a teaching vehicle in the community.

MAGIC Magazine
6220 Stevenson Way
Las Vegas, NV 89120

(702) 798-0099

Web site: http://www.magicmagazine.com

MAGIC Magazine is the largest-selling magic periodical in the world. The monthly magazine contains feature stories on the art of magic, in-depth interviews with magicians, and new tricks and effects from some of the most creative minds in magic. It also includes magic news, editorials, and product reviews.

McBride's Magic & Mystery School

3132 Shadowridge Avenue

Las Vegas, NV 89120

(702) 697-7002

Web site: http://www.magicalwisdom.com

McBride's Magic & Mystery School is a place where magicians can go to learn, practice and perform magic in an intimate setting with many of the world's best magic teachers. The school offers classes and seminars for students of all skill levels and interests.

Society of American Magicians (SAM)

Society of Young Magicians (SYM)

P.O. Box 2900

Pahrump, NV 89041

(702) 610-1050

Web sites: http://www.magicsam.com; http://www.magicsym.com

Founded in 1902, the Society of American Magicians (SAM) is a worldwide organization dedicated to the art of magic. The Society of Young Magicians (SYM) is its youth branch, serving young people ages seven to seventeen who are interested in learning and performing magic. SYM has local "assemblies," or chapters, throughout the country.

Web Sites

Due to the changing nature of Internet links, Rosen Publishing has developed an online list of Web sites related to the subject of this book. This site is updated regularly. Please use this link to access the list:

http://www.rosenlinks.com/MAG/Presto

Alexander, Lloyd. *The Rope Trick*. New York, NY: Dutton Children's, 2002.

Barnhart, Norm. *Amazing Magic Tricks: Master Level* (Edge Books). Mankato, MN: Capstone, 2009.

Carlson, Laurie M. *Harry Houdini for Kids: His Life and Adventures with 21 Magic Tricks and Illusions*. Chicago, IL: Chicago Review, 2009.

Charney, Steve. *Incredible Tricks at the Dinner Table* (Easy Magic Tricks). Mankato, MN: Capstone Press, 2011.

Clark, James L. *Easy-to-Master Mental Magic*. Mineola, NY: Dover Publications, 2010.

Fajuri, Gabe. *Mysterio's Encyclopedia of Magic and Conjuring*. Philadelphia, PA: Quirk, 2008.

Fullman, Joe. *Mind Tricks* (Magic Handbook). Richmond Hill, ON: Firefly, 2009.

Jay, Joshua. *Magic: The Complete Course*. New York, NY: Workman Publishing, 2008.

Kaufman, Richard. *Knack Magic Tricks: A Step-by-Step Guide to Illusions, Sleight of Hand, and Amazing Feats* (Knack: Make It Easy). Guilford, CT: Knack, 2010.

Kawamoto, Wayne N. *Picture Yourself as a Magician: Step-by-Step Instruction for the Street, Stage, Parties, Card Table, and More*. Boston, MA: Course Technology, 2008.

King, Bart. *The Pocket Guide to Magic*. Layton, UT: Gibbs Smith, 2009.

Mason, Tom, and Dan Danko. *Food Magic: How to Do Amazing Tricks with Ordinary Food!* (Top Secret Magic). New York, NY: Scholastic, 2007.

Mason, Tom, Dan Danko, and Jeff Fredriksen. *Amazing Illusions: How to Make the Impossible (Look) Possible!* (Top Secret Magic). New York, NY: Scholastic, 2006.

Schafer, Albert. *Illusionology: The Secret Science of Magic*. Somerville, MA: Candlewick, 2012.

Tremaine, Jon. *Amazing Magic Tricks*. Hauppauge, NY: Barrons Educational Series, 2009.

Turnbull, Stephanie. *Mind-Reading Tricks* (Secrets of Magic). Mankato, MN: Smart Apple Media, 2012.

Zenon, Paul. *Magic of the Mind: Tricks for the Master Magician* (Amazing Magic). New York, NY: Rosen Central, 2008.

INDEX

About the Author

Nicholas Einhorn is a "Gold Star'" member of The Inner Magic Circle. In 2011 he "fooled" two of the world's most famous magicians on the UK TV show *Penn & Teller: Fool Us*. He subsequently won a trip to perform alongside Penn and Teller in Las Vegas. Nicholas has won a number of industry awards for his work, including: The Magic Circle Centenary Close-Up Magician 1905–2005; F.I.S.M (World Magic Championships) Award Winner 2003; The Magic Circle Close-Up Magician of the Year 2002; and The Magic Circle Close-Up Magician of the Year 1996. Nicholas performs at events and parties throughout the world as well as uses his magic to build crowds for some of the world's largest companies at business trade shows and exhibitions. Nicholas is regularly invited to lecture at magic societies and conventions the world over. As a magic consultant, Nicholas has designed and created the special effects for several large-scale stage productions as well as being a consultant on several feature films. He also develops and markets new magical effects for the magic fraternity. To date, his illusions have been purchased and performed by magicians all over the world, including some of the biggest names in magic, such as Paul Daniels and David Copperfield.